These are not all poems b less ridiculous terms…it's just some of my thoughts.

START...

This is the second book in a series of three titled 'The Anxiety Diaries'. What began as a monthly blog post turned into something bigger and better. My hope is that this book resonates with you or someone you love.

Table of Contents (poems)

1. Present
2. Frozen Road
3. Gourd 1
4. Gourd 2
5. Smile
6. Costume
7. Spaces
8. Skills And Spills Of Pills
9. Mental Mess
10. Summer Writing
11. The Road (Un)Known
12. Rivers
13. Rain
14. S(h)e Loves Me
15. Questions
16. Sweaty Palm Psalm
17. Breathe
18. A Hero's Hike
19. Sunrise II
20. The Nomad And The Wanderer
21. Slash
22. Indio Road
23. Someone Else
24. Lost
25. Is That You Jod?
26. Woman v.s Body
27. One last breath
28. Mother
29. Storm
30. Not A Poem
31. 04.15.17
32. The Luxury Of Exquisite Panic
33. Happy

INTRO

"Joy can be shared with others, but grief can only be felt alone."

One of the beautiful things about being a writer is the ability to create my art all over the world. I am not confined to an office or path in life. In the first installment of this series I wrote the majority of the pieces in Ontario, and British Columbia in Canada.
In this second installment, however, I crafted each page of words everywhere from Las Vegas, to Toronto, to an RV in Indio, California. Taking inspiration from every word from those around me, and each sense of my being.
I feel this overwhelming bittersweet happiness and sadness about the travels I have been so fortunate to do while internally weeping at the thought that my father will never be able to see me thrive. I'm grateful to my mother for her presence in my life and support. But I wish every moment of my days that I could share this life with my dad for longer than I was able to. And that's the thing about grief, it's not linear or simple. There is no how-to guide and no real guidelines for any of it.

DEDICATIONS

To my family, Terry Gaudette, Ann Ray, Keith Gaudette, and Bruce Ray. This book is for my friends scattered across the globe who inspire and love me endlessly. Nelfam, which is home to some of the most magical beings in my world.

To my cats, yes…I am dedicating this to my cats…it's my book I'll do what I want to with it. Slash and Duff, you are my little beacons of light and balls of fur.

For the girls, the theys and the gays.

To my 11th-grade English teacher Adam, thank you for helping me to hone my craft and creativity. And for that one time that you allowed me to submit a painting instead of an essay.

This book is for anyone who has felt trapped in their own mind with no way to express that feeling. And for anyone who has felt the loss so great that they feel as though they may never be the same.

```
O P P M C H E E S E
T F R A L F A P B G
L E R C A F N O R N
O T R A R T N P U E
S L U R V O I S C L
S O R O Y J L V E S
L O T O N E A V L A O
E T C I B M B I P N
E E K K E I T H V V
P R L O V E U V T I
```

Present

I'm wrapped in a ragged cardigan, the fabric is hugging my skin like sand to water
I can hear the rain outside as it crashes onto the awning.

My hands are clutching a cup of tea so tight that I feel as though I could crush the vessel.

I can feel the warmth of it on my palms and in my body as the liquid slips like a hand to silk toward my stomach.

The room is dark, but there is a glow adjacent to me illuminated with fireflies outside of the window.

I am content.

I am aware.

I am present.

Frozen Road

Ahead, all I could see was an open road and snow-capped trees.
I wondered how each snowflake had fallen into the place it needed to be and if I was ever to do that?
Fall into the place I need to be that is.

Even as a child I had thoughts there, often too consumed within them to find a moment to seize, let alone a day.

I did not have the desire to jump into the water either, I had already felt like I was drowning in a pool of ideas of trying to be a normal person.

But today, at this moment, I am taking the time to wonder about these snowflakes, the frosted dancers in the air.

Gourd 1

Sully Halloween
A dried spooky gourd dances under the moon

Gourd 2

Taken up decline
A small fuzzy pumpkin on the skeleton

Fun fact: These two gourd poems are ones that I with no context nor asking for sent to Matthew Gray Gubler on Instagram.

We have never met, nor spoken.

Smile

The Sun glimmered off of her freshly licked lips. My body became littered with goosebumps as I felt her cheekbones on my fingertips.
Her rosy cheeks rose as her smile emerged and her eyes squinted.

Costume

Aren't we all wearing costumes?
A disguise of who we want to be?
Whom do we feel that we need to be?

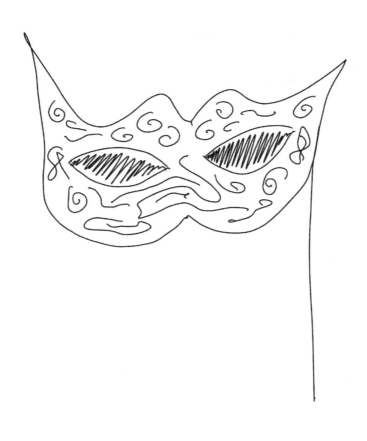

"That's the thing about life, you'll never make it out alive"

Spaces

Cracks in a foundation are caused by a broken-hearted creation
And
A
Love
Deviation.

Spaces

Needed as your soul swallows you whole and in their heart, you know that you are not the starring role.

S p a c e s

Skills And Spills of Pills

Clonazepam
Alprazolam
Lorazepam

I am Sam, Sam I am.

Diazepam.

Now, who am I?

I wonder and wish willingly as the wind whistles.

What am I?

A princess of a prescription pad?

No. I am calm.

For now.

Mental Mess

I'm surrounded by my own mess.

My clothing is littered around me, dirty dishes mocking me from my bedside table.

I would make the bed tidy but my anxiety ensures that I am not able to.

I have not brushed my hair nor my teeth in..days. I disgust myself, however, the thought of a shower sends me into a mental spiral.

MESS

SSEM

mess

mess

Mess

MESS

MESS

Mess

MESS

MESS

MESS

Mess

Summer Writing

The Summer sun sings.
A small magical box sings beyond the pencil.
Can't you feel it? Creeping its way into your body and mind like always.

The Road (Un)Known

The road - winding
My thoughts - I'm finding

I am in no way a wanderer, however, I was never given a map to this life. My path is just as unknown as my future and the road before me.

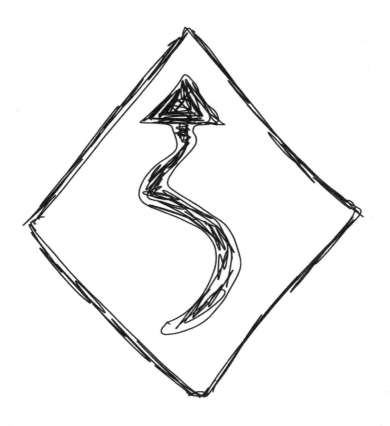

Rivers

Liquid summertime
An anxious river splashes
before the woman

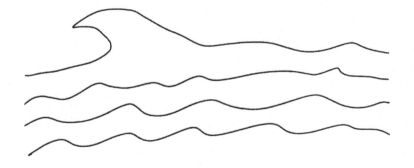

Rain

her regrets were dust.
they swathed her
in an thirsty pall
of failed passions
and missed chances.
she was heaving for breath
when a gentle rain
washed them down.

(S)he Loves Me (not)

The petals from the flower fall harder to the ground than I did for you.
Sepals hugging the representation of your desire for me, they're so loud and yet you make not even a coo.

It took me years to realize that the petals falling were merely showcasing how little we did not water our garden, a lack of effort comparable to few things. I allowed the final piece of the flower to fall with the loudest ping.

Questions

At the age of fourteen I began to have many thoughts of mine end in a question mark.
I questioned my faith, my ambitions, and my sexuality as if I had discovered them again for the first time.
Is there a god? I asked, do the angels hark?
Why do we go to church and ask for forgiveness just to sin again?
There were notions of Catholicism that were not adding up for me, my father was very ill and my deep sadness was erupting and becoming evident that it was more than teen angst. How could there be a god when it seemed like I would be spending my whole life seeking a moral bargain?
I could not spend the remainder of my days eating bland crackers and praying to something I did not believe in, later on I would go from Nikki Gaudette to Nikki Sin.
I had always thought that there was something wrong with me, that I was only supposed to like boys. I was to let them pull my pigtails and act out to show me that they liked me.
Girls to me had always been a thing of beauty and wonder, so powerful and mighty in their femininity.
But I couldn't be gay…right? I have to like one or the other with no questioning in sight.
I was to have children, and marry a man who couldn't satisfy me sexually nor emotionally with my closest female friends in hideous dresses.
White dress, white veil, white picket fence with my shining armor donned white knight.

However, just as my disdain at the idea of leading out my life devoted to god and the church, I knew that I could also not spend it on a scale of sexuality and desire that was so linear. So set in stone as if Medusa had a hand in it.
So what was my "label", as if I were a can of soup, where in the world did I "fit"?
It would be years before I could admit to myself that I was a bisexual, and many more to admit it to others.
The human desire to be loved, to love and to have faith in something other than your soul can be so complex yet so simple.

But now begs the question, do I deserve what I desire?

Kiss

Love

heat

LGTBQ*

Sweaty Palm Psalm

Their formation occurs in slow motion becoming as wet as any ocean.

One by one they become a focus of your mind as the lead as they go from feelings of fear to a bead.

Cold, clammy, and a feature of a rabbit. No relief even when you use a towel to dab it.

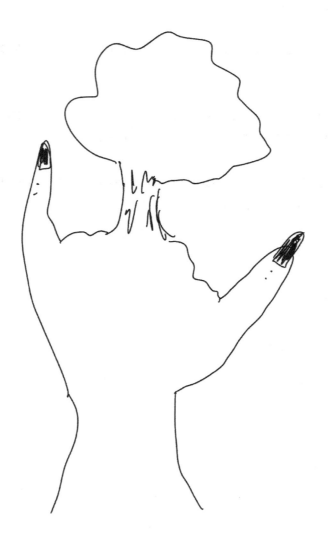

Breathe

It gets harder and harder to do every day, piercing my throat and veins like daggers. The steps I attempt to take trickle down my legs as a stagger.

A Hero's Hike

I cannot help but stop and ponder the treacherous trek.
Down, down, down into the darkness of the mindful wreck.
Gently it goes - the unreliable, the unsafe, the punic.

How peaceful is this moment of flurries and fury?

I cannot help but stop and look upon my past and what she was unable to do.
Down, down, down into the darkness out of view.
Gently these thoughts they go - the humorous, the foolish, the cuckoo.

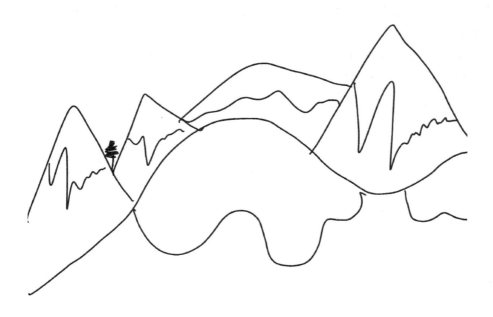

Sunrise II

Sunrise
Warm, inviting
Dusking, warming, yearning
Ever so sanguine
Dawn

The Nomad And The Wanderer

See the calling of the Nomad,
I think he's angry at the keypad.

He finds it hard to see the pen,
Overshadowed by the chilling Parisienne.

Who is that sneering near the wolf?
I think she is weary that her thoughts will soon engulf her.

She is but a scared Wanderer,
Admired as she sits upon a patch of moss to ponder.

Her soul is just a like a lover,
It needs no gas, it runs on cloud cover.

The two approach a mountain,
Words and tears welt up like a fountain.

The Nomad shudders at the heavy snow
He wants to leave but she does not want to go.

And so off they go on their separate ways,
Both spend their days under the same rays.

Slash

```
         be
paws               be
large             cat
very angry large
black, big, epic
 ever so rotund
 quite meddling
decidedly large
black, fond, big
positively angry
 black and white
 black, mean, fat
 black, esoteric, tender
 its fat belly shift, forte
 soft mitts pinching, swiftly
 puny maulers pinching, swiftly
 smallest hands swiping, swiftly
 subgross hands filching, swiftly
  littlest mitts filching, swiftly
  its petite hooks lifting, swiftly
   micro hands abstracting, swiftly
    dwarfish mitts filching, swiftly
    its teeny hands hooking, swiftly
    young mitts purloining, swiftly
    its petty paws lifting, swiftly
    its rotund belly shifting, forte
     corpulent abdomen moving, forte
     its teeny paws hooking, swiftly
     ever so fat venter shift, forte
     subatomic paws swiping, swiftly
     its mysterious middles rumbling, conservatively
    ever so inscrutable centres rumbling, conservatively
 quite large ever so large hearts rumble, conservatively
    big cat   colorful eyeballs murmuring, conservatively
       vomit                                    all deep
                                                  feline
```

Indio Road

She had the windows rolled down with her hand surfing along the flows and motions of the air out of the car, you could smell hints of burned matches and proper liquor from an improper bar.
Two spirits as free and flowing as the birds that glide above them howling into the wind in the night like banshees. An enigma of sound, time and space created as far as they could see.
The destination mattered less than the miles driven and moments created.

"Am I just to accept that this is the way things will always be?"

Someone Else

I wish I could be someone else.
I wish it were as simple as that, to transform into someone who was better and stronger.

I wish I could be someone else.
Someone who knew the end of the path that she was taking, someone who could keep her head out of the clouds and in the game.

I wish my skin felt like my own and not fabricated by society and others' views of me. I wish that my image did not feel crafted by the notions of those around me.

If I could just be someone else…I would have so much more love for myself, and see myself the way that everyone else seems to.

Lost

Is there no map to the soul and mind? I cannot seem to hold on to the direction of where I am going or should be going. Why does it seem so much easier for others to get through life?

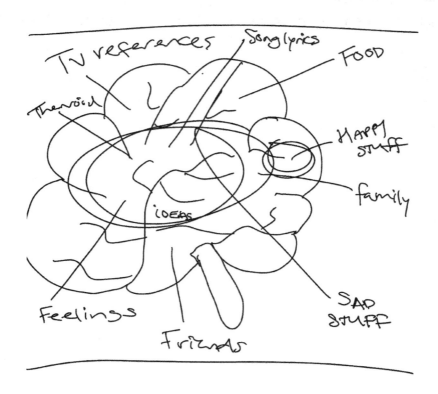

Is That You Jod?

I envy those of the spiritual mindset, the belief that there is someone, or something out there. I cannot grasp the idea that in a world filled with so much pain, my brain and heart filled with so much agony, that there is some greater power out there seeing all of that occur with no desire to intervene.

666

Woman vs Body

I spend a lot of my days at war with my mind and despite the work that I do to be the victor of that battle, I remain trapped with thoughts unkind.
I am constantly, continually, and consistently conned by the conflict with the mirror as my trigger. The battle zone for all of this is that of my own figure.
The best I can do is put on a performance from day to night, and play pretend as if I am not in an internal fight.

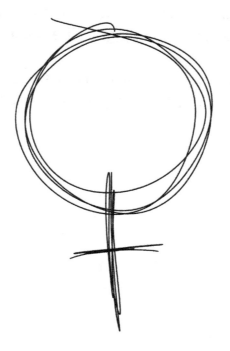

One Last Breath

May purgatory come upon us
Not but a smile
A moment, a day (March 15th, 2017)
Tour blue
A moment, a day
One last breath

(Why couldn't you have more?)

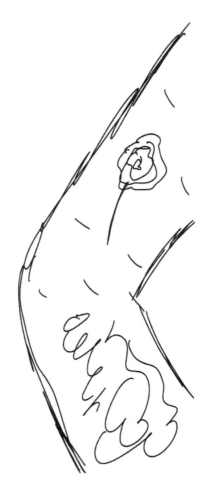

Mother

There are many ways to describe you and I'll admit I haven't always used the most kind of words.
You're resilient, loving, and you're brave, and the notion that I have ever thought otherwise is absurd.
Thank you for cushioning my falls to rock bottom and reminders of who I am and could be.
Mama I love you, and I hope that this is something that you can see.

Storm

Beautiful, haunting
the god glory of thunders
The torrential rains

Not A Poem

This will not rhyme or make you happy as the reader. I just…I miss my dad and I cannot scream it into the world enough, so this time I will type it.

This is not a doodle.

04.15.17

There are many days that I cannot remember but moments that are etched so vividly in my mind, some that left me devastated. If you put me under some sort of cartoon detective lamp I would be unable to tell you what happened at my high school graduation, or what led to my love desperation.

What I can remember is every touch, smell and sound of March 17th in 2017. I wish it were the day I fell in love for the first time or realized a dream. Instead it is the day my life changed and my father's ended, it is the day I often need to sink my nails into my fist to jolt out of it's memory. I was always told that time would heal me, but I am still in pain with it ending incrementally.

The Luxury Of Exquisite Panic

Her uniform was a tiny black dress, riding slowly up her thighs as she made her way through the city that would continue to break her heart like the men of her past.

Headphones so secure in her ears with the comforting sounds of the same songs she has had on repeat for days, developing her personality for the next 4 minutes based on the book she read last. Main character? Not quite but not the story's villain or victim. Every once in a while she let out a prehistoric scream to get the anger out of her system.

As she approaches the front door of her home she holds her breath with the anticipation of a release.
A release of the clenching of her jaw, her fists, and breath leading to peace. Peace behind her door, where she is free to sob, and prepare for her next venture to the outside with a sheer panic increase.

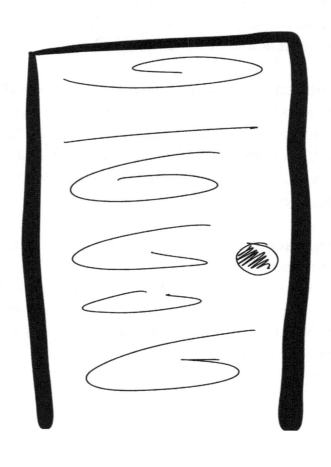

Happy

The title of this book perhaps gives the illusion that I am never happy, and for a while I thought I may never be.

This thought occurred well before March 15th of 2017 and I feared there would be no end in sight for me to see.

I think that right now…I am happy.

So you made it to the end, no Grover at the end of this one sorry.

END.

Made in the USA
Middletown, DE
20 October 2022

13165881R00046